EDGE BOOKS

The Real World of Pirates

THE PIRATE CODE

LIFE OF A PIRATE

By Liam O'Donnell

Consultant:
Sarah Knott, Director
Pirate Soul Museum
Key West, Florida

D1455423

Capstone
press®

Mankato, Minnesota

Edge Books are published by Capstone Press,
151 Good Counsel Drive, P.O. Box 669, Mankato, Minnesota 56002.
www.capstonepress.com

Library of Congress Cataloging-in-Publication Data
O'Donnell, Liam, 1970–
      The pirate code : life of a pirate / by Liam O'Donnell.
      p. cm.—(Edge Books. The real world of pirates)
      Summary: "Describes the daily lives of pirates, the code of conduct they lived
by, and the punishments they faced if they broke the rules"—Provided by publisher.
      Includes bibliographical references and index.
      ISBN-13: 978-0-7368-6424-4 (hardcover)
      ISBN-10: 0-7368-6424-5 (hardcover)
      1. Pirates—Juvenile literature. I. Title. II. Series.
G535.O36 2007
910.4'5—dc22   2006001004

Editorial Credits
Aaron Sautter, editor; Thomas Emery, designer; Jason Knudson, illustrator; Kim Brown,
      production artist; Wanda Winch and Charlene Deyle, photo researchers

Photo Credits
Art Resource, NY/Erich Lessing, 6–7
The Bridgeman Art Library/*Marooned* (detail), 1909 (oil on canvas) by Pyle, Howard
      (1853–1911) © Delaware Art Museum, Wilmington, DE/Museum Purchase, 22–23
Delaware Art Museum, Museum Purchase, 1912, Howard Pyle, 1853–1911,
      An Attack on a Galleon (detail), 1905, oil on canvas, 5
The Granger Collection, New York, 26
Image courtesy of Arjan Verweij, 15 (both)
The Image Works/Topham/Fotomas, 9
Mary Evans Picture Library, 16–17
North Wind Picture Archives, 19
Paul Daly, 27
Peter Newark's Historical Pictures, 10–11, 12 (top), 13 (both), 18, 20
Richard T. Nowitz, 8
Rick Reeves, 12 (bottom), 14–15, 24, 28–29

1 2 3 4 5 6 11 10 09 08 07 06

TABLE OF CONTENTS

CHAPTERS

FEATURES

Chapter One

HARD LIFE

On the night of April 1, 1719, a small rowboat approached the large English cargo ship the *Bird Galley*. The men in the rowboat were cold, tired, and wet.

The captain of the *Bird Galley* called out to the men on the small boat. Did they need help? Were these men friends or enemies? The men in the boat answered with a blast of their guns. These men were not friends. They were pirates, and the *Bird Galley* was under attack!

Learn About:
- Raiding ships
- A pirate's life at sea
- Working together

Pirates sometimes used small boats to sneak up behind large merchant ships.

Damp and Diseased Ships

Raiding ships like the *Bird Galley* was the highlight of piracy. But pirates led rough lives the rest of the time. Their days were filled with hard work, and they lived in miserable conditions.

Pirates were almost always wet and cold. In the 1700s, wooden ships leaked a lot, even in good weather. During strong storms, cold water often poured into a ship's lower levels. Many pirates suffered from muscle cramps because their clothes and blankets were always cold and wet.

Pirate ships were crowded, dirty, and usually filled with disease. Ships were often infested with beetles, leeches, and rats. These pests carried diseases that spread quickly. Sometimes half of a ship's crew could die from disease. Pirates burned a form of tar called pitch on the ship. It made a thick black smoke they hoped would chase away the pests. But it didn't work very well. The diseased pests stayed anyway.

Why did pirates choose to live in such miserable conditions? Because the Pirate Code guaranteed that they would all be treated equally. It also promised an equal share in what they all wanted—treasure!

EDGE FACT
Some pirate crews were so sick from disease that when they took over a new ship, they raided the medicine chest before the treasure chest!

Working Hard for Treasure

Pirates made their living by stealing. They sailed the oceans looking for merchant ships carrying gold, spices, weapons, and other gear that they could steal.

But to succeed in getting the treasure, pirates had to do a lot of work. The Pirate Code made sure everyone did their job and that they worked well together. With a lot of hard work and cooperation, pirates kept the ship sailing smoothly and ready for their next raid. By following the rules of the code, many pirates became very rich.

Pirate ships were busy places. Every pirate had a job to do, such as scrubbing the deck, manning the sails, or repairing battle damage.

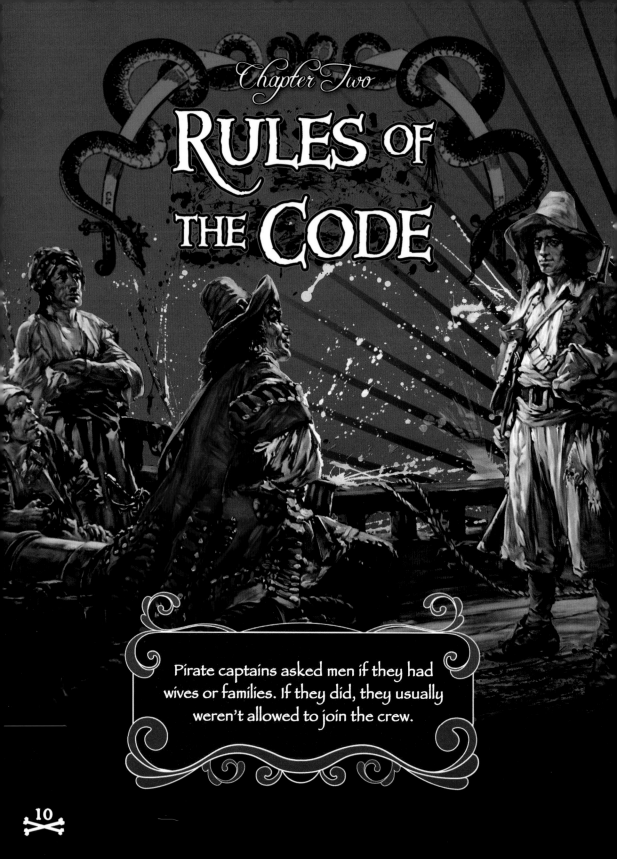

Chapter Two

RULES OF THE CODE

Pirate captains asked men if they had wives or families. If they did, they usually weren't allowed to join the crew.

Pirates led wild lives of robbing and killing. It's hard to imagine that these cutthroats would follow any rules. But the rules of the Pirate Code made sure pirates treated each other fairly and that no man betrayed his shipmates.

Joining a Pirate Crew

Every pirate ship had its own code. Before any man joined a pirate crew, he had to first sign the ship's code and swear his loyalty over the Bible or an ax. This was called "going on the account." The pirate then had the right to a share of any treasure taken. But by signing the ship's code, he also risked jail time or even death if he was ever caught by the authorities.

Learn About:
- Becoming a pirate
- Pirate women
- Gambling

Equal Say

One rule of the Pirate Code gave each pirate a vote in where they sailed and what ships to attack. Before a captain charted a course or fired a cannon, he had to check with his crew. If they didn't like the captain's idea, they wouldn't do it.

Articles of Agreement,

Made the 10th Day of October, in the Year of our Lord 1695. Between the Right Honourable RICHARD Earl of BELLOMONT of the one part, and Robert Levingston Esq;

AND

Captain William Kid,

Of the other part.

WHEREAS the said Capt. William Kid is desirous of obtaining a Commission as Captain of a Private Man of War in order to take Prizes from the King's Enemies, and otherways to annoy them; and whereas certain Persons did some time since depart from New-England, Rode-Island, New-York, and other parts in America and elsewhere, with an intention to become Pirates, and to commit Spoils and Depredations against the Laws of Nations, in the Red-Sea or elsewhere, and to swear with such Goods and Riches as they should get, to certain places by them agreed upon; of which said Persons and Places, the said Capt. Kid hath notice, and is desirous to fight with and subdue the said Pirates, as also other Pirates with whom the said Parties. That for the purpose aforesaid the said Capt. Kid is to have the Command. It is agreed between the said Parties. That for the purpose aforesaid the said Capt. Kid is to have the Command of the said Capt. Kid, shall be forthwith bought, whereof the said Capt. Kid is to have the Command. Now these Presents do witness, and it is agreed between the said Parties,

...

Pirates were always on the hunt for new ships to attack.

Women Pirates

On many ships, the code had a rule banning women from coming aboard. Many pirates thought women were bad luck. The code promised punishment for any pirate who tried to sneak a woman onto the ship.

But not every pirate ship banned women. Some women actually became pirates. Anne Bonny and Mary Read were two of the most famous. They sailed with "Calico" Jack Rackam during the early 1700s. They usually dressed as men, and they fought as fiercely as any man. Even when their ship was captured in 1720, Bonny and Read continued to fight when all the men hid below deck.

Anne Bonny

Mary Read

Pirates often settled their differences with violence. If a pirate felt someone was cheating, he might try to kill the man.

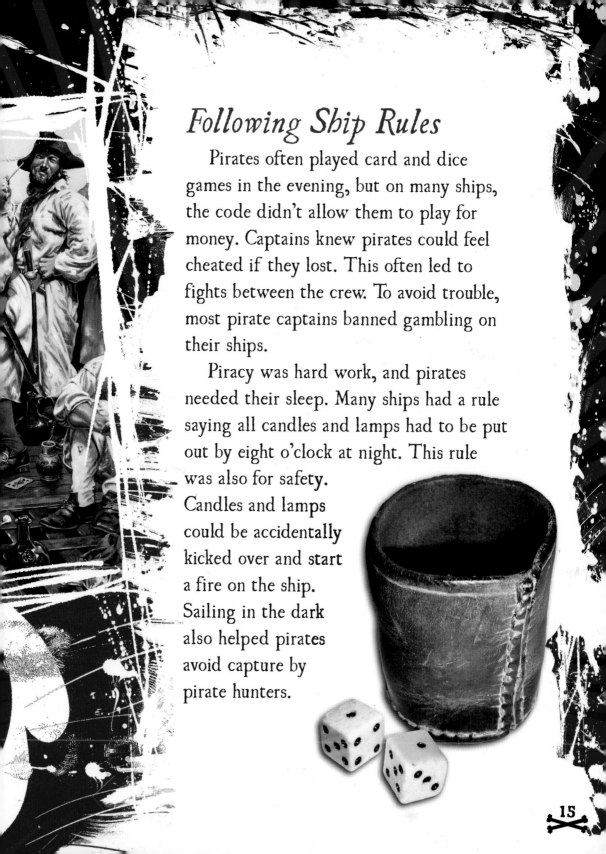

Following Ship Rules

Pirates often played card and dice games in the evening, but on many ships, the code didn't allow them to play for money. Captains knew pirates could feel cheated if they lost. This often led to fights between the crew. To avoid trouble, most pirate captains banned gambling on their ships.

Piracy was hard work, and pirates needed their sleep. Many ships had a rule saying all candles and lamps had to be put out by eight o'clock at night. This rule was also for safety. Candles and lamps could be accidentally kicked over and start a fire on the ship. Sailing in the dark also helped pirates avoid capture by pirate hunters.

Pirates didn't attack at first sight. They usually waited to see if a merchant ship was carrying anything of value first.

Chapter Three

RULES OF COMBAT

Pirates were always on the hunt for more treasure. They usually needed to fight to get it. The rules of the Pirate Code helped pirates succeed in battle to steal ships and treasure.

Hunting Down Treasure

When pirates spotted a merchant ship, they didn't attack right away. The captain first watched it from a safe distance through a small telescope called a spyglass. He wanted to see if the ship was carrying any gold or valuable cargo.

Learn About:
* Hunting merchant ships
* Fighting battles
* Dividing the treasure

Pirates followed merchant ships for hours or even days before attacking. They wanted to see how well armed a merchant ship was before they tried to attack it. If the merchant ship carried a large crew or a lot of weapons, the pirates wouldn't attack. They wouldn't risk their lives if they thought they couldn't easily get the ship's cargo.

Ready to Fight

Pirates always had to be ready for battle. The Pirate Code stated that every pirate had to keep his weapons clean and ready for action. If a pirate let his sword get rusty or his pistol become jammed with dirt, he would face punishment.

During a battle, every pirate had to stand and fight or risk breaking the Pirate Code. If a pirate ran away from battle or refused to fight, he would be punished when the fight was over.

Pirates were fierce fighters. They used many weapons, including flintlock pistols and curved swords called cutlasses.

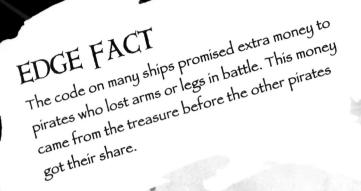

EDGE FACT

The code on many ships promised extra money to pirates who lost arms or legs in battle. This money came from the treasure before the other pirates got their share.

After a successful raid, pirates divided the treasure according to their position on the ship.

Dividing the Treasure

After a battle, it was time to divide the treasure. According to the code, each pirate received a share based on his job. The more important a pirate's job, the bigger his share of the loot.

The captain had the most important job. He was in charge of the ship, so he usually received two shares of the treasure.

The quartermaster assisted the captain. He made sure the captain's orders were followed on the ship. He also was in charge of distributing supplies and making sure the stolen booty was divided equally. His share was usually equal to the captain's.

The gunner kept the ship's guns working and ready for battle. The gunner often received one and a half shares. Most pirates did not have special jobs. They received only one share.

Chapter Four

BREAKING THE CODE

Pirates were feared across the seas for their cruel crimes. But pirates who broke the Pirate Code were also punished, often with death.

Left Behind

Sometimes captains of merchant ships were marooned when pirates stole their ships. But pirates who broke the Pirate Code could also be marooned. A marooned person was left behind on a deserted island, far from any other people. He was given little food or water, and usually a pistol with only a single shot. If he didn't die from starvation or thirst, he usually took his own life.

Learn About:
- Marooning
- Pirate punishments
- Walking the plank

When a pirate was marooned, he had little hope of rescue. He usually took his own life before dying of thirst or starvation.

Pirates who stole from their shipmates paid a heavy price for their greed.

Cruel Justice

Pirates rarely stole from each other because they faced cruel punishments if they were caught. One punishment for thieves was to cut off their noses or ears and put them ashore. Men missing bits of their faces were sure to be recognized. They were likely to be captured by the authorities and punished for their crimes.

Another way to punish a thief was to tie him to the mainmast of the ship. The guilty pirate was left without food or water for days. He was often beaten badly. Sometimes the other pirates circled around him, jabbing at him with their daggers and swords. They then rubbed salt or vinegar into his open wounds. Pirates rarely stole from their fellow pirates more than once.

Pirates who killed a crewmate received a terrible punishment. They were sentenced to the "Murderer's Swim." The guilty pirate was tied to the body of the murdered man and then thrown overboard and left to drown. It was a strong warning to everyone that they should get along with their shipmates.

EDGE FACT

Walking the plank is the most famous pirate punishment, but it never happened! There are no documented cases of pirates making their prisoners walk the plank.

Flogging

Flogging was a painful and effective punishment. It kept pirates from fighting with each other or breaking other minor rules. This punishment called for a lashing with a special whip called the cat-o'-nine-tails. It had nine ropes attached to a handle. Each rope had hard knots tied into it, and sometimes fishhooks or other sharp objects were tied to the ends.

Pirates sentenced to flogging had their shirts ripped off to expose their bare backs. Flogging caused large, painful cuts that took a long time to heal and sometimes became badly infected. Most pirates made sure they never had to suffer this punishment.

The Pirate Code made sure pirates lived and worked well together. Without a set of rules, pirates wouldn't have been very successful.

Learning from the Pirate Code

Some of the punishments for breaking the Pirate Code were as cruel as the pirates who broke them. But the rules were made for the benefit of all the pirates on a ship. The code helped pirates become rich by making sure they worked well together, and that they each received their fair share of the treasure.

Though they were thieves and murderers, pirates still had to live by the rules to be successful. By studying the Pirate Code, historians have learned a lot about how pirates once lived and the world they lived in.

Glossary

booty (BOOT-ee)—another name for treasure

infected (in-FEKT-uhd)—to be contaminated by germs that cause illness or disease

mainmast (MAYN-mast)—a tall, strong pole in the center of a ship that holds the ship's main sails

marooned (muh-ROOND)—to be left alone on a deserted island

quartermaster (KWOR-tur-mass-tur)—a ship's officer who makes sure the captain's orders are carried out and that supplies are distributed among the crew

spyglass (SPYE-glass)—a small telescope; a spyglass makes faraway objects appear larger and closer.

starvation (star-VAY-shuhn)—a condition of suffering or dying caused by a lack of food

vote (VOHT)—a choice you make based on your views

Read More

Clibbon, Meg, and Lucy Clibbon. *Imagine You're a Pirate!* Imagine This! Toronto: Annick Press, 2002.

Steele, Philip. *The World of Pirates*. The World Of. Boston: Kingfisher, 2004.

Williams, Brian. *Pirates*. A First Look at History. Milwaukee: Gareth Stevens, 2005.

Internet Sites

FactHound offers a safe, fun way to find Internet sites related to this book. All of the sites on FactHound have been researched by our staff.

Here's how:

1. Visit *www.facthound.com*

2. Choose your grade level.

3. Type in this book ID **0736864245** for age-appropriate sites. You may also browse subjects by clicking on letters, or by clicking on pictures and words.

4. Click on the **Fetch It** button.

FactHound will fetch the best sites for you!

Index